# PROVING NOTHING TO ANYONE

Publishing Genius Press
Baltimore, Maryland
www.PublishingGenius.com

Copyright © Matt Cook 2013 All Rights Reserved
First printing June 2013

Cover image and author portrait by Friese Undine
Book design by Adam Robinson

ISBN 13: 978-0-9887503-2-6

"Foothills Panic" and "A Long Story" appeared in the *Evergreen Review*; "My Wife's Car" and "Solitude" appeared in *Everyday Genius*; "At the Bodega" in *Faultline*; "Conventional Raindrops" in the *Hawaii Review*; and "New Poem Thingy" in *ExpressMilwaukee.com*.

# PROVING NOTHING TO ANYONE

**MATT COOK**

Publishing Genius Press
Baltimore 2013

Also by Matt Cook:

*The Unreasonable Slug*
*Eavesdrop Soup*
*In the Small of My Backyard*

# CONTENTS

*ONE*

| | |
|---|---|
| 1 | The Dry Cleaner Calls Up |
| 2 | Conventional Raindrops |
| 3 | A Long Story |
| 4 | Wilkie |
| 5 | After Prolonged and Inconclusive Thinking |
| 6 | A Spanish Cement Mixer |
| 7 | Commitment to Excellence |
| 8 | Sestina with Love and Socks |
| 10 | The Above-Average Dead Person |
| 11 | Scott's Fingers |
| 12 | Gordon Park Pub |

## TWO

15 Foothills Panic
16 Something Beguiling
17 The Drunk Man's Hat
18 I Don't Have All Day
19 Ron Had Arranged to Watch Cindy's Dogs
20 Unchanged from Ancient Times
21 Suppressed Laughter
22 Dwarf Seahorse Habitat Fragmentation Parade
23 Excellent Taste
24 Not Hitting a Road Worker
25 The Moose

## THREE

29 My Wife's Car
30 On the Road (with Wife)
32 123
33 Solitude
34 Interesting Things
35 An Impossible Question
38 Minimal Damage
38 Jesus in My Hair
40 The Man with No Sophistication
41 Hopeless Somersaults
42 My Dead Friend
43 The Emotional Center

## FOUR

| | |
|---|---|
| 47 | We Drove into Town |
| 48 | New Poem Thingy |
| 49 | In the Bodega |
| 50 | You're a Minor Poet Standing Near the Frozen Spinach |
| 51 | Inexhaustible |
| 52 | Sestina with Common Cold |
| 54 | Somewhere in Particular |
| 55 | Unpredictable Fallout |
| 56 | Not Really My Problem |
| 57 | They Probably Laughed |
| 58 | Forgotten |

## FIVE

| | |
|---|---|
| 61 | Ordinary Catastrophes |
| 62 | Duane Duane |
| 63 | Listening to a Man |
| 64 | When My Ears Are Cold |
| 65 | Cough Drops |
| 66 | In a Cloud that has a Funny Name |
| 67 | Poetry with Death and Salt |
| 68 | An Awful Sound |
| 69 | Leadership Crisis |
| 70 | Lost in Friendly Waters |
| 71 | Irksome Particulars |

For Liddy and Hazard

"For goodness sake, honor poetry—as a good, intelligent old woman, whom one may drop in on sometimes, so as to forget for a moment the gossip, the newspapers, and the cares and bothers of life, to be diverted by her pleasant chattering and her stories; but to fall in love with her is unwise."

—Alexander Pushkin

# ONE

# THE DRY CLEANER CALLS UP

The dry cleaner calls up and says he's taking responsibility for my pants.
Well that's fine coming from him.
The doctor has a vested interest in my mother's skin eruptions,
The psychiatrist is happy when I'm sad,
The cartographer essentially wants us to get lost.
The restaurant supply store might as well be a secret
Society as far as the hound with the droopy ears is concerned.
The hair dresser apologizes to the poet, but the reverse almost never happens.

## CONVENTIONAL RAINDROPS

You're a conventional man walking down
An ordinary street with a questionable haircut.
An ordinary woman broke your conventional heart.
Questionable skies are giving way to conventional raindrops,
Thoroughly average raindrops, raindrops that are hardly worthy of your attention.

You're walking home right now because
You were attacked by black flies at the punk rock coffee shop.
You found yourself taking the black flies personally,
Which is always an important signal.

The bread factory is making below average bread but it smells fantastic.
People from nowhere who used to live somewhere have decided to live here now.
All they talk about is somewhere and they never mention nowhere.
Dirty little birds the size of doorknobs are living above the drugstore.

You're a second-rate man living under an assumed name in a first floor apartment
But it's a nice apartment and the windows look out on the park.

Other than the windows looking out on the park,
Things are generally wrong everywhere.
Your shoulder is malfunctioning.
You're running low on contact lens solution.
You have a full head of hair and you're unemployed,
But you could pass for a bald man with a job.

# A LONG STORY

Remember that time you drank vodka and grape soda
And you vomited purple vomit on your white sport coat
And the photographer came by and took a photograph of you?
The black and white photograph of the purple vomit on the white sport coat.

I remember five minutes ago like it was yesterday.
When you were a boy, I remember, you had a strong dislike for passages
In a book where a character was making his way through the dark.
You resented printed words that wanted you to visualize not being able to see.

Remember that invisible fence you installed along your father's property?
You wanted to keep your father's dogs from running into the street.
You told me once that you had a problem with your invisible fence.
I said, What's the problem with your invisible fence?
You said, It's a long story.
I said, I don't want to hear a long story about an invisible fence.

# WILKIE

Her feet hurt really bad and
She was sick of John Singleton Copley
And the holes in the drywall needed spackling.

She fouled up the vinyl letters really bad last time and
Todd made her do the whole thing all over again.
Todd said she ruined nine hundred dollars worth of vinyl lettering.
For that paragraph on the wall—talking up Copley's *directness and vitality*.
Every show they hung seemed to have some guy with *directness and vitality*.

There was also an old man who worked at the museum,
And every day he emptied his colostomy bag
Off the side of the loading dock.
That was as brilliant as anything she'd ever seen.

It was Copley's *palette* that made her sick.
That same palette over and over again.
*Boy with a Squirrel* in that same dumbass palette.
Todd said *Boy with a Squirrel* had an *atmospheric quality*.

She liked very much the *backs* of those paintings, though.
Everybody had seen a Monet or a van Gogh,
But she had seen the *backs* of those paintings.

# AFTER PROLONGED AND INCONCLUSIVE THINKING

After a hard day killing rabbits with a hammer,
I could really go for a condescending
Article about a family without running water.

This room is the color of a room.
I feel I'm on the lunatic fringe of tomato lettuce and cabbage.
After prolonged and inconclusive thinking,
I pronounce you a drunken saint with synthetic earmuffs.

I bring the full force of my poetic resources to the gasoline station.
I, who reconciled the contradictions of the school lunch program.

An old lady and the old man walk past, but they walk in single file.
I still do not really believe there's a skeleton inside of me.

There's organ failure and there's organ grinder failure
And there's you're dead in the ground failure
And there's rainbow peppermint lip balm failure.

Good luck getting a straight answer from
The counselor at the home for colorblind children.

I now pronounce you an old lady and an old man.

# A SPANISH CEMENT MIXER

I was in Spain one time, and I saw a cement mixer.
An ordinary cement mixing truck, driving down a street in Spain.
And I thought, what do you know about that? A Spanish cement mixer!
The vision was profound and disorienting.
I wasn't *prepared* for a Spanish cement mixer.
I hadn't *anticipated* a Spanish cement mixer.
*Who knew* they mixed cement in Spain?
Of course! Of course they mixed cement in Spain!
Perfectly good cement being mixed all the time in Spain!
I felt *hoodwinked*—I felt *dangerously unschooled* in Spanish cement!

# COMMITMENT TO EXCELLENCE

During a dinner party at my house
A woman leaned back into a candle
And caught her long hair on fire.

She did not notice this right away, but I noticed it—
But at that very same moment,
I was in the middle of telling a really good story,
And I knew the punch line of the story was only seconds away,
So I continued, and only after the punch line was delivered,
And after the appreciative reaction of the room,
Did I finally let the woman know her hair was on fire.

The woman was not seriously harmed,
And she ended up writing me a letter of recommendation.

# SESTINA WITH LOVE AND SOCKS

My wife can't find any of her socks.
The things keep disappearing—it's a sign
Of something or other, like dead worms on the sidewalk.
Socks moving uncontrollably through the chaos of space.
We trust the socks are in good hands.
When you score nothing in tennis they call it love.

How does the substitute teacher explain love?
The police report on the missing socks
Is about as useful as a ghost giving you a hand
Job as you're working to sign
The great mysteries into law, the gravitational forces in space—
The road to hell is paved with sidewalks.

Nobody complains enough about the sidewalks.
Instead, they go outside and fall in love
And circle the block looking for metaphysical parking spaces.
There's no satisfying explanation for the disappearing socks.
There's no leading alternative theory, no sign
Of life on other parking lots—you throw up your hands.

When the big hand gets on the one, and the little hand
Gets on the six, put your worst foot on the sidewalk.
Rob yourself with a ballpoint pen and sign
Away your claims and rights to the above-stated love,
And then kiss all your socks
Goodbye and have your remains sent into space.

Please print with blue or black ink in the provided space.
What's the point of all those fingers on your hand?
Inside an old T-shirt I find one of your socks,
Like finding a buffalo nickel on a sidewalk,
The potato salad that dare not speak its love,
Incomprehensible regulations on no-parking signs.

Please do not take this as a sign.
Do not write below this space.
When you score nothing in love they call it love.
Someone will write a popular song about holding your hand.
The neighbor will throw her husband's clothes on the sidewalk.
I want to hold your socks.

# THE ABOVE-AVERAGE DEAD PERSON

Big misunderstanding with powerful man behind desk.
Almost-dead butterfly falling through aluminum tractor trailer.
Disorganized lecture notes discovered by protagonist in greenhouse.
It's *his* greenhouse, he can discover whatever he wants there.
Accumulation of unread periodicals from almost-dead intellectuals.
Uncontrollable hiccups during drunken sex.
City councilmen momentarily confused by ad hoc furniture situation.
Who has *time* for the miscellaneous demands
Of the average dead person—or the above-average dead person?
Ivan the Terrible tortured and killed his own son.
Peter the Great merely killed his son.
The outside world is making strange noises.
Peter the Great died of a urinary tract infection.
It was probably a *great* urinary tract infection.

# SCOTT'S FINGERS

In a large city, I went into a café to get out of the rain. There was a broken man sitting at the bar and we talked for a while. He said he was a musician, and he wanted me to know that he was a successful musician, that he knew *a hawk from a handsaw* and all of that—that he'd *been around the block* and all of that. There was a thunderstorm of unexpected beauty outside and we watched that for a while. Then he told me about his friend Scott. He liked Scott, he said. He would give Scott *the shirt off his back*, he said. But he would never allow Scott to touch his guitar. He said that Scott's fingers were very sweaty, and not only that, the sweat on Scott's fingers was not your ordinary sweat, but rather some weird sort of *Scott sweat*. He said the one time he allowed Scott to play his guitar, the sweat from Scott's fingers *deoxidized* the metal of the guitar strings. That's what he said: the sweat from Scott's fingers deoxidized his guitar strings. Then we talked some more, and he said that he and Shirley MacLaine were good friends. I'm pretty sure he was lying about that, but I'll bet Shirley MacLaine's *real* friends are not much better.

# GORDON PARK PUB

You got drunk, passed out,
Woke up under the coin-operated table,
Wearing only one contact lens,
Peanut shells stuck to your back,
Unable to remember the good joke Phil told,
Remembering only the punch line that involved *kinesiology*.
Vague recollections of the party the night before,
Some birthday girl everybody hated,
Awful buffet food, unidentifiable macaroni salads,
An argument concerning Harry S. Truman,
Whether or not he really needed to vaporize those women and children,
Well, if you put it *that* way, somebody said.
But now the sun is coming in through the windows,
Like it wants everybody to go to work or something,
And you think they're starting to love you at this place.
They treat you like a half brother,
And they give you cigarette-flavored yogurt and Spanish newspapers.
You wouldn't call this no fun.
You've had no fun, and this is more fun than that.

# TWO

# FOOTHILLS PANIC

There's a grocery store at the foot of the mountain
Where they misspell the name so you remember it better.
You drive past failed motels and successful dead chickens.
The cavemen live in houses and the housewives live in boxes.
There's nowhere good to stay except the abdominal pouch of a marsupial.
There's water leaking from a man's car, strawberry ice cream from a woman's ear,
The sound of one branch of philosophy breaking.
There goes the zoologist with his renegade speculation on sleeping bats—
It's nice to see an ineffectual man in his natural habitat,
Refusing to cooperate with local authorities,
Acknowledging only the iridescent plumage
Of the common rain gutter bird.
They have to put *something* at the foot of the mountain.
Lurid banner at gardening center reads: *Cypress Mulch Madness.*
The bread at the supermarket is always up against the wall.
The stockboys are laughing at your descent into irrelevance.

## SOMETHING BEGUILING

If the birds sang in English,
The morning would be unbearable.

I woke up feeling hopeless and was comically jolted into happiness
By simplistic, tragic optimism found in an op-ed column
Which confirmed my pessimistic superiority
And I felt better right away.

It was the sort of morning where one goes to a café and
Orders a meal associated with a later period in the day.

I made small talk with a man who made even smaller talk with me.
We talked about the relative merits of bicycle locks
Then the discussion broadened into the nature of human trust.

Then the man said something intelligent and
I responded by saying something clever and
He replied by saying something absorbing and
I countered with something maddening and
He came back with something beguiling.

The beautiful tropical birds
Eat the same thing every day.

# THE DRUNK MAN'S HAT

The poetry comes easily in the morning,
Not because the head is clear, but because the head is confused.

The cat's brain is the size of a strawberry
And he only uses ten percent of it.

The ants in the pantry have a way of micromanaging the marshmallows.
I had a dream where I wrote a poem about making a lithograph:

A line drawing of a town drunk at mid century.
He's a broken down alcoholic, but he's still wearing a suit and a fedora.
Only the brim of his hat is flipped up, bubbles coming from his mouth.

This was back when degenerates still tucked in their shirts—
Back when we still paid attention to the shirttails of degenerates.

He's talking to a security guard in a blue windbreaker.
The conversation isn't going well.

The drunk man is saying something like:
Give me the awful chemicals I need to clean this hat.
If you can do that for me, I would certainly appreciate it.
If not, I can find something else to appreciate.

# I DON'T HAVE ALL DAY

The moon needed a new shirt to go with his old tie. So the moon took a bus downtown to a respected haberdashery. When the moon entered the shop, he saw a jackal working behind the counter. The moon said, "I need a new shirt to go with this old tie. Do you follow me?" The jackal said, "Yes, I follow you, but to obtain such a shirt I must journey to the bottom of the shirt world and speak with the pig." The moon said, "I don't have all day." And the jackal said, "Ease up cowboy, you'll get your shirt." So the jackal journeyed to the bottom of the shirt world but he made no effort to contact the pig. The pig was known to do excellent work, but he took his time doing it, and the jackal didn't need that right then. So instead, he sought out the spider mom. The jackal said to the spider mom, "The moon needs a new shirt to go with his old tie." The spider mom then began to talk, but the talk was completely unintelligible because it wasn't really talk at all but more like spit, and soon the jackal's face was covered with spider mom spit. The jackal then abandoned the spider mom and pushed further toward the bottom of the shirt world. He stayed in a motel down there and he stole the largest bath towel they had. "I will make this bath towel into a shirt and sell it to the moon," the jackal cried, stuffing the bath towel into his rucksack. But when the jackal returned to the haberdashery, the moon was gone. This made the jackal furious and he resolved to make a new shirt anyway, just to spite the moon. This is why today the jackal has such a distinctive coat and why the moon is so out of fashion.

# RON HAD ARRANGED TO WATCH CINDY'S DOGS

Ron had arranged to watch Cindy's
Dogs when Cindy was out of town.
Then Elizabeth came to town
And wanted to stay at Cindy's place.
Cindy's place was available, of course,
Because Cindy was out of town.
But now with Elizabeth staying at Cindy's place
It no longer made sense for Ron to watch Cindy's dogs.
Elizabeth was very pretty and Ron would surely behave
Foolishly around her and make things awkward for Elizabeth.
But nobody had the heart to say that to Ron
So they told Ron that Elizabeth would watch Cindy's dogs,
Which was a lie, because Elizabeth was a party girl
And she could not be trusted to look after someone else's dogs.
So instead, Marguerite was enlisted to look after Cindy's dogs.
Cindy's dogs were well taken care of.

# UNCHANGED FROM ANCIENT TIMES

He wanted to see trees that were thousands of years old.
He wanted to lie on the forest floor and
Look up and see a view that was unchanged from ancient times.

So he went deep into a national forest and
Then he returned and I asked him how it went.

He said he took mushrooms and freaked out and
Smeared peanut butter all over his Volvo wagon.

# SUPPRESSED LAUGHTER

The stupid little things that make you happy—
The stupid little things that make you sad.
Literature will always need people standing around
With their hands in their pockets.

If you pass the woman who looks like a folded shirt, you've gone too far.
Go to where the young man smokes cigarettes near the propane tanks.

I don't know about you, but it's looking like our independence
From England is probably going to stick.
What kind of weirdo compares a woman to a summer's day?

I never really got to know my mother—
The fact that I was her son always got in the way.
Where does the energy of suppressed laughter go?
Why not a family car
Powered by the energy of suppressed laughter?

# DWARF SEAHORSE HABITAT FRAGMENTATION PARADE

Life is short but this day will never end.
The police officer is seventy percent water.
The police officer has a way of making the sandwich shop less fun.
Let's discuss dwarf seahorse habitat fragmentation until he goes away.

He's not the first authority figure to make a sandwich shop less fun.
This poem has flies laying eggs in all the wrong places.
Let's avoid geopolitical metaphors when badmouthing a sandwich shop.
I'm honoring you by feeling sorry for myself.

This poem has flies laying eggs in all the wrong places.
When the poetry fails, I blame distant relatives.
I'm honoring you by feeling sorry for myself.
Let's pay a lot of money for an unattractive machine that causes cancer.

When the poetry fails, I blame distant relatives.
This poem could be more fun if we put balloons and things around it.
I would like to pay a lot of money for an unattractive machine that causes cancer,
Inspiration follows the afternoon spent with socially useless individuals.

This poem might be good if we put balloons and things around it.
Life is short but this day will never end.
Inspiration follows the afternoon spent with socially useless individuals,
Eating carry-out food from a rectangular foam box thing.

Do not use geopolitical metaphors when badmouthing a sandwich shop.
The police officer makes the sandwich shop less fun.
Discuss dwarf seahorse habitat fragmentation until he goes away.
The police officer is seventy percent water.

# EXCELLENT TASTE

In Norway it's possible to get whale as a topping on pizza.
I never ordered such a pizza,
But when the judgmental delivery man brought it to my door anyway,
He acted like it was my fault there was whale on a pizza in Norway.

I was new in town and I inquired as to where I might go to find self pity.
He said I could find self pity at any of four convenient locations.

I met a woman who told me a raccoon bit off her index finger.
Her arms were folded as she spoke, so I could not confirm or deny her claim.
The woman with the folded arms who presumably lost an index finger to a raccoon
Talked very fast and said many bold and impressive things.

Her ideas were mostly stolen from others,
But she had excellent taste,
And she stole only the most beautiful ideas.

# NOT HITTING A ROAD WORKER

There's a dream I have of broken glass in my mouth.
I'm in a car accident, my head goes through the windshield,
And there's broken glass in my mouth.
Then I'm in a bathroom for some reason.
I'm coughing and hacking bloody fragments into a sink or a bathtub.
I'm being very careful, very conscientious, about where my bloody fragments go.
This is a relatively new dream of mine.
I had gone most of my life without ever dreaming of broken glass in my mouth.
And they say people don't change.

I'm a middle aged man half asleep on a couch in an advanced western democracy.
Can you see this book of poems from outer space?
Could this book of poems fetch even one cigarette in prison?
The short answer is no.

The sign says ten thousand dollar fine for hitting a road worker.
As though you need an *incentive* not to hit a road worker.

I always thought not hitting a road worker was its own reward.

# THE MOOSE

We were in the woods in Ontario, walking around, minding our own business, when we chanced upon a moose. It was a real live moose all right, standing about twenty feet away. *Oh my god, look! A moose*, one of us said. *Whoa, I can't believe this, a moose*, said someone else. *Holy shit, a moose, just right over there*, someone said. And we all stood there motionless, transfixed, trying to be as respectful as possible to the moose, trying to savor the moment. *This is so cool, a moose!* someone said. *I had a feeling we might see a moose*, someone said. *This is just so great, will you look at that thing?* Ten or fifteen minutes passed this way, and we were all still standing there, in awe of the moose. *Wow, look how big he is*, someone said. *Be quiet, don't startle him*, someone said. *I never knew they were that big*, someone said. This went on for another five minutes or so, all of us standing around flabbergasted at the sight of the moose. *This is really incredible, an actual moose*, someone said. Eventually, after another volley of these sort of remarks, one of us, I believe it was my brother, said, *Well, we just can't look at him all day*. And with that we walked away, with all the moose we'd ever need.

… THREE

# MY WIFE'S CAR

I was out for a walk one afternoon
When I saw my wife's car parked across from the film department.
You feel a kind of existential panic when you see your wife's car somewhere.
My grandfather said death is like looking at your house from across the street.
It's probably something like that.

You walk past a row of meaningless automobiles,
And suddenly there's your wife's car—what do you do?
You can't just walk past your wife's car.

She had twenty-two minutes remaining on her parking meter.
I have the key to her car, so I decided to wait.

I opened the door and sat down in the passenger's seat.
I knew she'd be happy to see me because we have an excellent marriage.

I sat there with the windows rolled down.
I noticed an oak leaf hydrangea in somebody's front yard.
I never even knew what an oak leaf hydrangea was
Until my wife told me what an oak leaf hydrangea was.

Then I saw her in the distance approaching the car.
I was enjoying the situation, the childish suspense.
But then she came closer, and I could see she was crying.
She opened the door and she put her arms around me.
She said, "I'm so glad you saw my car."

# ON THE ROAD (WITH WIFE)

Almost hit bicycle near creek crossed by Coronado,
Serviceable Vietnamese food Amarillo,
Overheard plans for foolish remodeling scheme,
Treated with suspicion by bookstore clerk New Mexico,
Transferred feelings about my cat to pigeon in town square.

Saw selfish jackrabbits in state park,
Urinated near Spanish ruins,
Tall grass blowing in wavy psychedelic manner,
Initially felt sorry for horse standing alone in field,
Then saw companion horse nearby previously obscured from vision,
Witnessed cow fornication.

Heartbreaking craft jewelry salespeople,
Ambiguous depressing European couple,
Large greedy oak tree hogging sun nutrients from smaller trees,
Bullet shell casing in parking lot not encouraging,
Legless man at bus stop alongside man with legs at bus stop.

Bought coffee from windblown hippie,
Saw cat eating a lizard,
Saw two lizards fucking then third lizard appeared and broke up fucking,
Amounting to a sort of weird lizard jealousy,
Saw goats, ponies, and anti-social peacocks.

Wife's big mouth leads to room upgrade,
Talked to religious man with yellow tinted shooting glasses,
Intermittent online checking of Wisconsin gubernatorial recall,
Talked to man whose father sold tires,
Talked to man who saved dog from criminal abuse,
Sat by charming cement water fountain.

Spinach tofu enchiladas,
Hassle over incorrect monetary denominations,
Tragic border patrol search of immigrant family,
Small girl holding fishbowl with goldfish,
Wife suddenly knowledgeable about thunderclouds.

Rise late to sound of clinking recycling bottles,
Lifesaving hangover breakfast,
Solitary man on side of road carrying elk antlers,
Museum guide with unfortunate skin complexion.

Lively bus station scene involving impulse chewing gum purchase,
Man on pay phone telling story of incarceration,
Hotel with expired elevator license,
Unfathomably annoying bar patron,
New colloquial expression for defecation learned.

Unethical irrigation practices discussed,
Insane pecan grove on one side of road, desert on other,
Adorable hitchhikers with dogs and guitars nevertheless bypassed,
Unnecessary deep fried food at romantic dive bar,
Pool cue accidentally disrupts muscle man at adjacent table,
Fall asleep to unmemorable TV.

Guacamole on riverbank under mud swallow nest,
Confronted cottonmouth water moccasin snake thing,
Committee dispute over options in snake situation,
I lobby for more cocktails,
Full moon,
Wife reads William Faulkner.

## 123

A passerby
Misapplying Aristotle
In Liechtenstein.

A fruit fly
Living in a bottle
Doing just fine.

# SOLITUDE

That's an awfully grand word for sitting alone at a kitchen table.
There's a fly going around and around and around the room.
He lands for a second on somebody's thank you note.

The microwave oven sounds like a very small fourth of July.
A reproduction of Willie Nelson's voice is coming through the vestibule.
It seems to be saying, Don't knock arsenic in the drinking water until you've
    tried it.
Let's be thankful we don't have to be thankful.

Then a moment's silence, then a mother's ambiguous voicemail.
It triggers a memory of a counterclockwise boyhood.
A bird flies into our garage in Illinois.
The bird walks out the side door with a rubber band in his beak.
My mother holds my hand like it's the last swordfish burrito on earth.

# INTERESTING THINGS

My friend brought some interesting things over to my apartment.
His backpack and his briefcase were full of interesting things.
Where did you get all those interesting things? I asked.
I got them in different places, he said.
I know another man who has access to interesting things, I said.
Sometimes interesting things fall from the sky and they land in different places,
 he said.
I had no idea there were so many interesting things, I said.
When something compares favorably to something else, he said,
That makes it an interesting thing, but it's also interesting
When something compares unfavorably to something else, he said.
Sometimes my mouth is full of interesting things, he said.
Did you grow up around interesting things? I asked.
Yes, there were interesting things on my father's side,
But on my mother's side there were mostly different places, he said.
Are we doing everything we can to promote interesting things? I asked.
He said nothing.

I wanted to understand more about interesting things.
I wanted to ask him if it were possible to define interesting things.
But I knew well that he distrusted precise definitions.

# AN IMPOSSIBLE QUESTION

Every time the gas company sends a worker to my house,
The guy gets here and all he wants to talk about is *gas*.
Why can't the gas company send someone *well rounded* to my house?

An impossible question is a nice thing to have around sometimes.
You tell me you pisshead—Is this pencil sharpener ordinary or extraordinary?

Every thirty-six months I have a nervous breakdown,
And then I forget who I am, and then some time passes,
And then I remember who I am, and it keeps me young.

A submarine crew of poets would be a mistake.
The fish in the ocean have no fresh water to drink.
Has anybody ever thought of that before?

# MINIMAL DAMAGE

He suspected that we liked him ironically,
But really we liked him sincerely,
But he never got past his initial suspicion
That we liked him ironically,
Which, to be fair, contained a grain of truth.

He lived alone in a small room and smoked a pipe and read Elizabeth Bishop,
And when you thought about him that way, he was lovely.

Sometimes, though, he would offer to buy you a beer,
And it would seem like a kind gesture,
But it was actually just a scheme
So that you would feel obligated to sit with him
While he discussed the shortcomings of your work.

He managed to quit smoking cigarettes for a while,
Until one day he backed his automobile into another automobile,
Which caused only minimal damage and yet
He went hysterical and justified a pack of cigarettes.

He gave me a manuscript of his unfinished novel
And the moment he was out of my sight
I put the manuscript in a drawer and never looked at it again.
I was certain my opinion of him would be lower if I read the manuscript.
I was only trying to protect him.

People ten years younger than him couldn't stand him.
People twenty-five years younger than him saw him as a kind of broken genius.

Sometimes, though, you could not listen attentively
When he began to paraphrase literary biography
And you would feel bad for him
And you would bring him a basket of popcorn.

We often wished that he were happier,
But had he been happier,
We probably never would have met him.

## JESUS IN MY HAIR

When I was in high school
There was this kid McNally
Who had an idea for a TV show called
Jesus in My Hair.

It takes place in a barbershop in Los Angeles,
And the barber is played by Desi Arnaz Jr.
What happens is the second coming of Jesus Christ
Lands in the alley behind the barbershop, and
Desi Arnaz Jr. takes him in, and
Jesus Christ hangs around the barbershop
Making a lot of snappy, Christ-like rejoinders and so on.
But then one day he bumps his head really bad and
He forgets that he's the second coming of Jesus Christ,
And Desi Arnaz Jr. has to keep reminding him,
Making a lot of stirring pep talks or whatever,
So that Jesus can rise to whatever occasion is called for and
Get somebody out of a jam that week.

I think that's how it went.
It was a long time ago.

Oh, and the show opens with one of those theme songs
Where the whole premise of the show is
Summarized in this kind of goofy ballad number.

So this guy McNally is in his forties now,
And I wrote him the other day, and I said,
Remember Jesus in My Hair?
Why don't you rewrite Jesus in My Hair?
And he acted like he was beyond the whole thing now,
Which really bummed me out,
Like he had outgrown Jesus in My Hair.

# THE MAN WITH NO SOPHISTICATION

He wanted to introduce me
To his friend who had no sophistication.
So he called his friend with no sophistication and
Told him to meet us at a café.
Every time the door would open
I would say, Is that the man with no sophistication?
And it never was.

Then the man with no sophistication called on the phone.
He said today wasn't a good day for him.

## HOPELESS SOMERSAULTS

My best friends all have rocks in their heads.
They ram cotton swabs into their eardrums for the laughs they can get.
They classify minerals incorrectly, and they take their time doing it.
These are the invisible, odorless, forgettable memories.

There was a perfectly good owl sitting in a tree.
An invisible, odorless, forgettable owl.

We startled the owl away with the sound of grand jury testimony.
The hopeless somersaults through introductory paragraphs,
The blanket involved in behavior unbecoming of a blanket,
The Human Resources lady living in a sea chest under the storm windows—
Suddenly every mule was a horse in particular and an ass in general.

The slip-on shoes, the slip-on socks, the slip-on teeth—
Everything is *slip-on* when you come right down to it.

I misunderstood my mother's misunderstanding of *General Hospital*,
Which amounted to a sort of *Very General Hospital*.

# MY DEAD FRIEND

I can still hear
My dead friend's voice
In my mind's ear.
It's a lovely dead friend voice—
It still makes me happy when I'm walking to work.
He made comfortable people uncomfortable,
Which always brought me comfort.
He died in the middle of a magazine subscription,
Like a bird dying of old age in mid air,
The philosopher killed by the falling turtle.

I once had a dream that my dead friend
Threw me down the elevator shaft
Of the English department building.

# THE EMOTIONAL CENTER

*for John Bensko—with no hard "feelings"*

Don't mess with me right now, I'm all stirred up with emotion, man.
I'm in a rage right now because I can't find my car keys.
Not only that, my Japanese fighting fish just went belly-up and died.
I'm really in despair about this, and there's all these emotions going through me, man.
My nervous system is really going to town on me with grief and things, man.
There's all this sugar in my bloodstream and my *glands* are emptying hormones everywhere.
The wind is blowing and it feels like the whole sky is full of emotion—
The whole neighborhood is full of emotion—
There's emotion backing up in the storm drains—
It's like an emotional sandwich, man,
And you've got all these emotional condiments,
And you take one bite and all this emotion oozes out everywhere,
And you've got emotion running down your chin and your arm.
Man, don't let me operate heavy machinery right now.

# FOUR

# WE DROVE INTO TOWN

We drove into town
To buy dead animals and beer
And white wine for the girls.
Cornwallis was driving the car.
An expert was talking on the radio.
Cornwallis knew more than the expert did,
Which made us feel strong.
We went to a farmer's market.
Cornwallis saw a man he wanted to avoid—
A minor character he knew from his high school days.
We bought a dead chicken and some new potatoes.
The dead chicken was expensive,
Because it was a chicken that had had a good childhood.
The girls requested a dead chicken that had a good childhood.
We drove away, successfully avoiding the minor character.
In the parking lot of the beer store,
We saw a dog leading an unexamined life.
The radio was now threatening to give away prizes.
We went inside and the dead chicken waited in the car.

# NEW POEM THINGY

All of the respectable nymphomaniacs had gone home over the holidays—
There was nothing to do except drink vodka in graveyards with competitive jerks.

Committing a misdemeanor can really build character sometimes.
The agoraphobics were under house arrest, which was fine by them.

We searched the parking garage of a very small Baptist college,
And we found many very small Baptists.

Nobody could tell which came first, the foreground or the background,
Or those snow shovels in back of the background or
Those Dumpsters at the edge of the foreground.

The Canadian geese in the quadrangle had impulse control disorder—
Everybody needed more critical distance from the decorative light bulb factory.

We couldn't find our car, and then we found our car,
And then we were sentimental for the days when we couldn't find our car.

We went for a drive, and we drove past houses we couldn't afford,
And then we drove some more, and we drove past houses we *could* afford.

# IN THE BODEGA

I saw a woman complaining about Jesus to her boyfriend,
While her boyfriend bragged about the reliability of his motorcycle—
Or maybe she was bragging about the reliability of her complaints to Jesus,
Or perhaps she was complaining about the reliability of her boyfriend.
The whole time I was just thinking about myself.
The owner of the establishment hated us all but he put up with us
Because we were buying things we really didn't need, which amused him.
My mother shouldn't feel bad that she drives me crazy, I thought.
Her mother drove her crazy; my great grandmother drove my mother's mother crazy.
There's a bug in my cat's ear; there's a tiny, tiny bug in my cat's bug's ear.
The saltine crackers at the market were under surveillance,
Which made no sense, except to men looking to protect their saltine cracker interests.
Right then a man walked in the store and I confused him for an old friend.
I'm sorry, I said, I thought you were someone else.
I *am* someone else, he said.

# YOU'RE A MINOR POET
# STANDING NEAR THE FROZEN SPINACH

You stop by the store to pick up your wife's favorite brand of beer.
Inside, an old woman goes out of her way to start a conversation with you.
You're wearing an overcoat that reminds her of an overcoat she once knew.
An old woman is allowed talk to you for as long as she likes.
You cannot tell an old woman to stop talking to you.
You're a minor poet standing near the frozen spinach.

When you get home you find that your wife is not home.
You go downstairs and transfer the laundry from the washer to the dryer.
A useful husband knows that the brassieres do not go in the dryer.
You remove them from the washer—
You hang them to dry on doorknobs throughout the house.

# INEXHAUSTIBLE

I need uninspired thoughts to help me fall asleep.
Average gray Warsaw Pact sort of thoughts,
Lukewarm oatmeal that falls short of lukewarm oatmeal standards,
Circular arguments at the rectilinear table,
Exhaustless, impossible to exhaust, inexhaustible.
I'll never fall asleep.
Boiled platitudes with couscous and pomegranate zest.
Impossible half dream about superfamily of eyeless mites
Forging a sense of community in lonesome pre-owned vehicle.

Disproportionate attention was paid to where George Washington slept—
Where James Monroe slept wasn't exactly chopped liver.

Now half awake nightmare about things that aren't even that bad—
Streets covered in garbage, beautiful garbage, the finest garbage.
Turn on light, read introduction to unfavorable biography of man with mustache—
Coconut vendors in market towns hostile to coconut vendors—

A bucket of clams and a pencil could not write this poem.

# SESTINA WITH COMMON COLD

Abominable snowman with common cold.
Much congestion in abominable head.
Drinking plenty of fluids from streams near fallen wood.
Living in dark cave, reading lonely monster newspaper.
Weather today not looking so good.
Snowman mentioning weather in snowman blog.

Have you seen abominable snowman blog?
Examines telecommunications during Cold
War, redistribution of wealth for common good,
Ironic commentary on shrunken heads
Of state, paper party hats folded from newspaper,
Lost art of ambiguity in bright snowy wood.

Abominable snowman's relationship to wood
Underrepresented in conventional blogs.
Wood begets paper, paper begets newspaper.
Baby snowmen, so to speak, recovering from common cold.
Ideas growing out of side of snowman's head.
Publicity for snowman generally not good.

Recontextualization of snowman myth not very good.
Public want fashionable monster lurking in fallen wood.
Abomination growing out of side of snowman's head.
Snowman making new enemies everyday on blog.
Ironic commentary giving way to strange head cold.
Washed up monster reading yesterday's newspaper.

Snowman go to town to buy newspaper.
Snowman find newspaper at store, newspaper look good.
Snowman say, "Hello, I have common cold."
Shopkeeper say, "Do you live in the wood?"
Snowman say, "I write important blog."
Shopkeeper goes mad and retreats into shrunken head.

Pitiful horn growing out of side of snowman's head.
Technicolor monster delivering prehistoric newspaper,
Singing lonesome ballad from prefabricated cave, writing furry blog,
Crawling onto hard funny ground, walking around, up to no good,
Abomination in distant valley of snowy wood.
Ambiguous monster loitering with common cold.

# SOMEWHERE IN PARTICULAR

Rays of sun not going anywhere in particular.
Flower shop in bankruptcy court where it belongs.

Fire department waiting patiently for fire to break out.
Fire department waiting around to be told to go somewhere in particular.

Scary man with tiny dog not allowed on bus except during dream—
Premium swivel laundry organizer disappears into a radiant fog.

# UNPREDICTABLE FALLOUT

Misadventures of disgusting water insect under plastic bucket,
Philosophical musings of park ranger on low sodium diet.

Unpredictable fallout from
Poorly worded fortune cookie
Crystallizes anti-union sentiment.

Open soars on forearm
Unexpectedly impress
The leading women of Philadelphia.

# NOT REALLY MY PROBLEM

The complicated girl who looked simple from across the room.
The simple girl who looked complicated from across the room.

Her father was Director of Fun Things for Confused People to Do.
He almost died once eating a Hawaiian pork chop—
Laughing uncontrollably, his mouth full of sparkling water.

He *did* die, eventually—of something other than a Hawaiian pork chop.
His obituary was in the newspaper.

The obituary of the complicated girl's father—
It was right next to the obituary of the guy who invented frozen French fries.

Her father died on the same day as
The guy who invented frozen French fries.

Through our insanity and our desperation
We accomplish as much as through our discipline.

I said, 'How does one really invent frozen French fries?'
She said, 'You know, that's not really my problem.'

# THEY PROBABLY LAUGHED

There was a spot on my blue shirt tonight.
A television news magazine program was also on tonight.
The spot on my blue shirt offered greater authenticity.

Warm soapy water became something I was searching for.
I'll bet they thought warm soapy water would never amount to anything.
They probably laughed when warm soapy water first came on to the scene.

Just because it takes courage to admit you're wrong doesn't mean that you're wrong.
I used to be young and drunk and stupid.
And then I became less young and less drunk and less stupid.
But I'm still pretty young and pretty drunk and pretty stupid.

# FORGOTTEN

I can't even stand to be in the same room with myself.
Something old something canned something borrowed something bland.
I'm reading a badly written book about a miserable man.
We don't even remember when we forgot this forgotten painter.
But misremembering is a mode of originality.
The underground room with the particle board and the poodle wallpaper.
You supply the blood and the sweat, I'll supply the tears and the poodle wallpaper.
Write about what you know about what people across town know.
My grandmother's favorite bird was the cedar waxwing.
Do you know what *your* grandmother's favorite bird was?

# FIVE

# ORDINARY CATASTROPHES

Do I need to remind you that the conversation
Never survives the journey from the dining room to the living room?
Would you rather be killed tomorrow,
Or eat wallpaper paste everyday for a year, and then be killed?
Is it just me or does time fly when you're ruining someone else's life?
Is it so hard to imagine driving intentionally into flashing roadway barricades?
Are you always so incredulous in the face of garbanzo bean-sized hail?
Am I the only one around here who sees any advantage in radioactive Scottish puppies?
Why must you walk the Piggly Wiggly parking lot with an affected Spanish gravity?
Is it not completely clear that your mother's brother's girlfriend's doctor's house
Is lousy with overvalued unappreciated intermediate-quality
Antiquarian tablecloths with no resale value?
Do you not understand what yesterday went through to bring us today?
Do you not understand what a difference a difference makes?
Doesn't everybody look forward to sitting alone, on the brink of suicide,
Waiting for porcelain figurines to arrive by mail?
Was the delivery boy so wrong to point out all the ways he was right?
Why were you so angry at the sound of the wind blowing in your ears?
Did you want the wind to sound *better* somehow?
Did you not appreciate what the wind went through to get where it was today?

# DUANE DUANE

He was in and out of institutions during the nineteen seventies. He was in group therapy sessions with a man who shot part of his face off. He wrote a song once about feeding saltine crackers to a duck. He wrote a poem where he rhymed Noxema and Iwo Jima. He watched a lot of television at the institution. He thought *Gilligan's Island* was real. He sincerely believed that *Gilligan's Island* was real. Let me explain this a bit more. He knew *Gilligan's Island* was a television show, that wasn't the point. He knew it was a television show with actors, that wasn't the problem. But he was convinced these actors were *forced, against their will,* to act out this show—that they were enslaved by television executives and forced at gunpoint, or through emotional blackmail, or whatever, to act out *Gilligan's Island* every week. This wasn't at all funny to him. And all of the madcap schemes the characters would contrive to get off the island, the smoke signals, the flying jalopies and so on, he believed these plots were really just *code* for us, the viewer, to go and save these people from this television show. He truly believed these actors were suffering deeply. He suspected they were being tortured. He was convinced the Skipper was blinking at him in Morse Code. He believed these things as much as you or I believe anything. This story isn't funny, but it's also funny. It's not *my fault* that this story is funny.

## LISTENING TO A MAN

I'm listening to a man
Describe a mountain range over the phone.
He went somewhere, apparently,
Somewhere that had a mountain range.
Now he's trying to describe
The mountain range over the phone.
He's fouling the whole thing up really bad.
This man obviously has
No business describing a mountain range over the phone.

## WHEN MY EARS ARE COLD

Everybody said she looked just like her mother,
But nobody could remember what her mother looked like,
So the evening was off to a bad start from the beginning.

I don't remember whether she threw the pumpkins
And I caught them and put them in the truck,
Or whether I threw the pumpkins
And she caught them and put them in the truck.

My brain doesn't work when my ears are cold.
A giraffe will clean his eyes with his tongue.
Why don't more sentient beings clean their eyes with their tongues?

Her bathtub was full of dirty dishes,
She had two kittens named after vice presidents,
And she stole interlocking floor tiles and rationalized it with Marxist dogma.

## COUGH DROPS

That crow on the sidewalk with his one bad wing
And his poorly understood song—
He's picking up a worm and he's making a big production out of it,
Using all of his crow motor skills and everything.
He's been making no sense for years now,
But he's getting worse and worse at it,
To the point where he's almost making sense somehow.
Such are the paralyzing contradictions that bloom
In the early spring under the telephone wires.

You feel tragic when the Walgreen's woman recognizes you.
You're not even at Walgreen's, you're under the telephone wires somewhere,
You're entirely removed from the Walgreen's context,
You're just trying to appreciate a crow,
But there she is, the Walgreen's woman,
The woman who sold you cough drops a while back,
Cough drops that were considered shocking by the standards of their day,
And now here you are, unable to live up to the ideals to which cough drops aspire.

You'd like to believe that your experience with cough drops
Is the definitive experience with cough drops,
The only true experience with cough drops.
You know this is impossible, but you also know
That somewhere out there is another person who might enjoy that idea.
Until you find that person you're no one,
You're just a confused man with high blood pressure
Warbling under the telephone wires.

# IN A CLOUD THAT HAS A FUNNY NAME

I'm up in a cloud that has a funny name,
You're down in the street with a plastic bag.
You're talking to a disoriented man in a blue watch cap.
I'm falling through the sky and it's painless and terrifying.

You're down in the street with an experimental rain poncho.
You're organizing unemployed window washers, or something.
I'm falling through the sky and it's painless and terrifying.
You're negotiating canned meat and durable goods.

You're telling the window washers what they want to hear.
Who will make the cakes and pies for tonight's disagreement?
You're negotiating canned meat and durable goldfish.
I'm falling through a cloud that's shaped like New Jersey.

You're speaking with authority about grades of motor oil.
Do you ever wonder what I'm doing, what I'm speaking about?
I'm falling through a cloud that's shaped like a dog wearing a hat,
Through a cloud that looks like an inferior teapot, or something.

Don't you ever wonder what I'm doing?
I wonder what you're doing with the man in the blue watch cap.
I'm falling through a cloud that looks like an old telephone.
I'm falling through a cloud that has a funny name.

# POETRY WITH DEATH AND SALT

When the small man dies in the large house
It gives you something to talk about at work.
When your wife finds poetry in your pockets
She doesn't even bother to read it.

It gives you something to talk about at work.
The obituary of the failed piano player gives you hope.
Nobody else bothers to read it.
Found at bottom of staircase with head injuries.

The obituary of the failed piano player gives you hope.
You're never too old to misinterpret Stravinsky.
Found at bottom of staircase with head injuries.
Killed by the awful sound of rich people clapping.

You're never too old to misinterpret the Constitution.
The press conference of the Undersecretary of Overdoing Everything,
The awful sound of rich people clapping,
The small businessman oversalting your food.

The Undersecretary of Overdoing Everything will not answer the question.
People with big houses will write books about people with small houses.
Your wife will find poetry in your pockets.
It gives you something to talk about at work.

# AN AWFUL SOUND

I'm disappointed with the ambition of the squirrels in this neighborhood.
They're squandering a lot of squirrel opportunities inside hollow trees.
I realize that ultimately this is *my problem*,
But what would a neighborhood be without an indignant old man?

I'm disappointed with the manhole covers around here.
They're a disgrace to manhole covers everywhere.

The flags are at half-mast and nobody will tell me why.
I write long sentences and I throw them away.

I probably write about squirrels too often, and I'm sorry about that.
I wish I were one of those guys who could
Write about squirrels *unapologetically*.

I saw a dead cat lying in the gutter.
That is, I'm pretty sure he was dead.
Either he was dead or he enjoyed lying motionless covered with flies.

Do you ever wonder where the Pepsi truck is going with all that Pepsi?

The intelligence agencies are floating through the sky,
Undermining hog-based economies—or is it the Mexican avocado mafia?

My wife's off somewhere *raising awareness* for something.
I'm not even sure what for.
I just know she's *raising awareness* for something.

Wait, there's an awful sound in the neighborhood.
It sounds like an overworked small engine, or the death of an important squirrel.

# LEADERSHIP CRISIS

The generalizations eventually die, just like everything else.
The streets all lead to the statue of the deadbeat dad.
The intersection looks like a totalitarian birthday cake—
Laboratory rats are going home to their laboratory rat families.

A three legged dog captured the attention
Of a struggling liberal arts college,
But then the attention became divided and
The dog was forgotten and the college went broke.

A claim supported by reason will not impress the desperado.
Unforeseen events will lead to unfinished practical jokes.
The unresolved leadership crisis at the punk rock coffee shop,
The napkin dispenser that broke America's heart,
The department store boycott that worked so well,
All of the rich greedy men went broke and
Volunteered at hospice centers.

# LOST IN FRIENDLY WATERS

There's a man inside of me that you wouldn't like.
But don't worry—I'm working on killing him off.
In order to kill him off, though, I need to employ
The man inside of me you wouldn't like.
I swear, though, once this is all done you'll like everyone inside of me.

Stars so small you cannot see them
Are living among us in the cupboards we never open.
What the omniscient narrator doesn't know won't hurt him—
The nonessential personnel are turning their pockets
Inside out as a protest against the stars living among us.

The Victorians were so uptight they ate bananas with a knife and fork—
But I suppose we ignore Victorian banana etiquette at our own peril.

I'm enjoying the limitations of my mind lately.
Are you enjoying the limitations of your mind lately?
Unfriendly submarines lost in friendly waters—

# IRKSOME PARTICULARS

When I say, I'm tired and my feet are cold,
And you say, Put on fresh socks and take a nap,
And I say, It's more complicated than that,
There are irksome particulars to be dealt with—
Well, is that the thanks *you* get for distorting reality for me?

There's a beer co-op in town, where you pay annual dues,
And you get a discount on beer, and you put in time helping out at the brewery,
Or on the loading dock or whatever,
And everything is carefully written down, or something like that,
And it all amounts to well intentioned drunks
Trying to remember how much good will everybody owes each other.

On some level we're all making omnidirectional headway
Tiptoeing through the toothpaste tubes,
Through a kind of golden age of overreaction,
Characterized by frisky and exuberant hand gestures.

I'm glad I met you when I was still an old man.
The love letter lost in the domed waste receptacle—
Is that the thanks I get for distorting reality for you?

*portrait by Friese Undine 2012*

Matt Cook is the author of three books of poetry (*In the Small of My Backyard, Eavesdrop Soup,* and *The Unreasonable Slug*). His work has been anthologized in *Aloud: Voices from the Nuyorican Poet's Café, The United States of Poetry,* and in Garrison Keillor's *Good Poems, American Places*. He lives in Memphis, TN.

www.ingramcontent.com/pod-product-compliance
Lightning Source LLC
Chambersburg PA
CBHW030448300426
44112CB00009B/1217